D1998057

Copyright © 2019 by CSB Innovations • All rights reserved

Smidgeon McGiggles is a mighty but very tiny sorcerer who lives in a cottage just outside the town of Fairyton.

This mighty sorcerer is famous for many reasons, and his inventions are just one. Many people don't know this, but Smidgeon McGiggles is credited for the invention of a light bulb that never burns out. How can this be, you must think? So I will tell you exactly how this invention came to be.

Chester, who is Smidgeon McGiggles' cat, has just one job to do, and that is to guard Smidgeon's spell book both day and night. One night while Chester was guarding the book, Chester heard a "Buzz" and a "Pop!" Next, the light bulb burned out. Chester dashed out of the cave to alert Smidgeon who, of course, wanted to see the burnt-out light for himself. "What a terrible time when the light bulb is not bright. I can fix this; I will think of a light bulb spell to recite."

The powerful sorcerer raised his wand and began to recite his spell "Light, light return to thee because brightness fills me with glee." The light bulb in the cave started to glow and glow, and still one hundred years later, that light bulb is still burning bright.

Laughter Potion

H2o

One day, Smidgeon decided to go to his family's surplus store, located far away in the town of Sumpkinville. McGiggles Surplus Shop sells everything; they say, "If we don't have it, it doesn't exist."

Just as Smidgeon was leaving, he walked out the door and said, "Flooper Pooper, I am in quite a scooper. Yesterday I drove too far, and then forgot to get gas for my car. With a spell, I can fix this mess, Mc Motor gas you need, but water is all I can see, so with my staff, I will add a little drop of water to thee."

And from that moment on, Smidgeon McGiggles never had to put gas in his car.

Yes, these inventions are very cool, but what makes Smidgeon so famous actually has nothing to do with his inventions. It's because of his spell book called "Ye Olde Book of Spells and Potions." This book contains powerful potion recipes; folks say that one potion can turn paper into metal, and there is another that helps you become a famous rock star.

With a book as powerful as his, you can see how Smidgeon McGiggles has many friends. Legends are told about some of Smidgeon's friends and how curiosity got the best of them. Legend says that one day they tried to get a sneak peek and then "Puff," no one ever saw them again!

Laughter
Potion

Owen Shingles was one of those friends, and it has been said that Owen loved to play dress-up; his favorite outfit was a suit of armor. One day, Owen grew tired of pretending and wanted a potion recipe that would turn his paper suit of armor into real armor.

Owen thought very hard and then decided to take a sneak peek at Smidgeon's spell book. As Owen walked into Smidgeon's cave, there at the end, he saw it "Ye Olde Book of Spells and Potions." It was glowing as brightly as it can be! He walked as quietly as he could be and turned the book to page three when suddenly, a thunderous voice echoed loud as can be!

"Owen, a sneaky peeky look you took into my secret book, a mouse you shall become for that look you took, and for every squeak you make, you will remember the Great Smidgeon McGiggles."

In an instant, Owen became a small grey mouse, and Chester being a cat, decided to play with that tiny mouse, and later the two became the best of friends!

Laughter
Potion

Laughter Potion

Another friend was Clara Thurton, a young apprentice of Smidgeon's, who desired fame. Just like others before, Clara thought she was sneaky enough to get a look at Smidgeon's book. But even though she walked on her tippy toes, Chester knows!

In an instant, Clara heard a click and a clack and then Smidgeon's thunderous words! "Clara, a sneaky peek you took, a lobster you shall become for that look you took inside my secret book, and for every click your claws make, you will remember the mistake you made."

Clara Thurton is famous no more; instead, she is a lobster that sits inside a bowl!

Laughter Potion

Laughter Potion

A world without spiders would be great indeed, at least that was what Cathy believed. In order to accomplish this, she would need a potion recipe. She went to the cave, hoping that she could get a look inside Smidgeon's book.

Silent as she could be, hoping that she would not be seen, Cathy opens the book again to page three. When suddenly, Cathy hears Smidgeon's voice echoing in the cave. "Cathy, a great apprentice, was thee, but you proved to be sneaky. For that peek you took into my book, an arachnid you will forever be. You must go now, and never come back to me!"

Cathy's tale is different because after her transformation, Smidgeon let her leave, and Cathy learned her lesson not to take sneaky peeks.

Cathy now spends her days writing potions and recipes of her own. Cathy's Cauldron is what her place is called, where she serves magical drinks and much more.

Laughter
Potion

Contributing Authors

Littel Authors

Contributing Authors

Odin Gale

Odin Gale: Is six years old and taught himself how to read when he was four. He loves dancing, especially Zumba, and wants to help everyone with everything. He has an enormous heart and is one of the most loving people you'd ever meet.

Sam R. Beach

Sam R. Beach: Is ten years old and she loves to be an artist. She loves playing with Littlest Pet Shops. She loves to draw and has also done some story writing. She has read the Harry Potter series along with many other books and authors. She is a Mine craft buff, and at her school, they promote writing and the arts.

Little Authors

Contributing Authors

Enrique Ortiz

Enrique Ortiz: Is twelve years old. He aspires to be a video game coder when he grows up. He enjoys Mine craft, Legos, and Dungeons & Dragons. He attends the school of Science & Technology. He enjoys playing video games, board games, swimming, camping, reading, and creating comics. He has a loving family.

NonaVee Gale

Nonavee Gale: Is ten years old and makes everything she does look easy, from playing soccer to dancing Zumba. Nonavee pours her heart into everything she does. She plans on helping run her food truck when she grows up.

LITTEL AUTHORS

CONTRIBUTING AUTHORS

JONAS NARVAEZ

Jonas Narvaez: Is seven years old and wants to be an artist, police officer, and a scientist! He loves to draw, create art, read, and play with friends. Jonas is generous, strong, and always willing to help someone in need.

ISABEL GALE

Isabel Gale: Is going to run a food truck when she grows up. She might only be 11 years old, but she has a talent for cooking healthy foods. She loves reading recipes and making them her own.

Gage X. Rivas

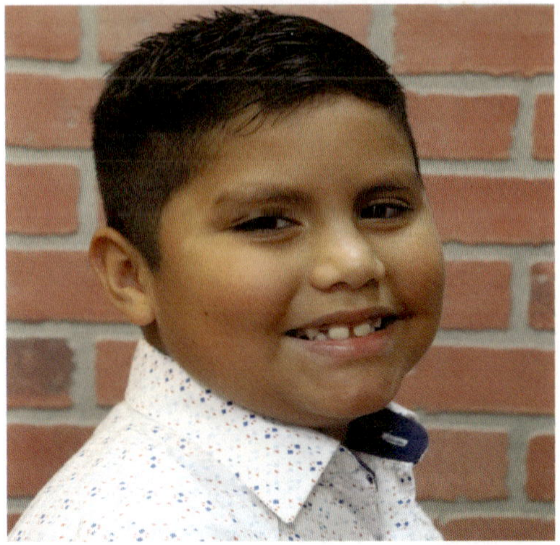

Gage X. Rivas: Is eight years old and wants to be a dog handler in the service when he grows up. He is a sweet, kind boy who loves his two dogs, Marshall and Merial. He loves to play baseball, video games, and ride dirt bikes.

Sebastian Narvaez

Sebastian Narvaez: Is eight years old, and he loves sports, especially Base-ball. When he grows up, he wants to be a teacher because he loves to read and help others learn. Sebastian is caring, strong, and holds empathy for others.

Your Children Our

Stories

CSB
INNOVATIONS

www.csbinnovations.com